The Amazing Life of Plants

Calling all aliens!

Are you planning a holiday to planet Earth?

Finn and Zeek are here to help.

'The Amazing Life of Plants'
Published by MAVERICK ARTS PUBLISHING LTD

Studio 11, City Business Centre, 6 Brighton Road,
Horsham, West Sussex, RH13 5BB, +44 (0)1403 256941
© Maverick Arts Publishing Limited February 2020

A CIP catalogue record for this book is available at the British Library.

ISBN 978-1-84886-677-5

www.maverickbooks.co.uk

Credits:
Finn & Zeek illustrations by Jake McDonald, Bright Illustration Agency
Cover: Jake McDonald/Bright, © Nigel Cattlin / Science Source / ardea.com
Inside: NASA Goddard / nasa.gov (7), **Ardea.com:** © John Daniels (8),
© M. Watson (11), © Thomas Marent (12), © Michel Rauch / Biosphoto (12),
© Nigel Cattlin / Science Source (13), © Pascal Goetgheluck (14), © Jean Michel Labat (15), © Mark Boulton (15), © Andrew George / natureinstock.co (15),
© Nigel Cattlin / Science Source (18), © Pascal Goetgheluck (19), © John Daniels (19),
© Jean-Michel Labat (20), © Kenneth W Fink (21), © David C Dixon (21),
© Franco Banfi / Biosphoto (22), © Brian Bevan (23),
© Steffen & Alexandra Sailer (24-25), © Bill Coster (27)

This book is rated as: White Band (Guided Reading)

The Amazing Life of Plants

Contents

Introduction	6
Life Cycle of Plants	8
Plant Structure	8
Smart Seeds	10
Flower Power	12
Super Stems	13
Survival Kit	14
Plant Givers	16
Breathe Easy	16
Food for Thought	18
Fitting In	20
Adaptation	20
Watery Wonders	22
Chilling Out	24
Quiz	28
Index/Glossary	30

INCOMING MESSAGE

Dear Finn and Zeek

We're planning a trip to Earth, and we'd love to discover why the planet looks so green from space. Is it covered in space snot, or something nicer? Hope you can help!

Yours,
Peebs and Pob
(Planet Mud)

Introduction

When you look at Earth from space, you can see two main colours – blue and green. The blue bits are water, such as oceans, lakes and rivers. The green bits are plants growing on land.

Plants on Earth include everything from a tiny blade of grass to a towering tree!

Plants provide humans with food, shelter, and the air they breathe!

There are nearly 400,000 different types of plants growing on Earth!

Life Cycle of Plants — Plant Structure

Most plants have three main parts - the roots, stem and leaves.

Leaves

Stem

Roots

1 Roots take up water and **nutrients** from the soil. They also help to keep the plant steady.

2 Water and nutrients travel through the plant's stem, to each part of the plant. The stem also helps to keep the plant upright even in windy weather.

3 Leaves help plants to make their own food. They use the sun's energy, clean air and water.

A plant stem acts like a straw sucking up goodness!

Life Cycle of Plants   Smart Seeds

Most plants grow from seeds. Seeds can be tiny or huge, but each one contains everything that's needed for a new plant to burst into life. Seeds can be fussy though – the conditions must be just right for them to start growing!

This seed has been resting during the cold winter. In spring, it gets exactly the right amount of warmth, water, sunlight and air.

The seed splits apart and a tiny root grows downwards into the soil. This is called **germination.**

The coco de mer palm tree seed can weigh up to 25 kilograms – that's about the same weight as six cats!

Leaves appear above the ground. This young plant is called a seedling.

A green shoot pokes through the soil, growing upwards towards the warm sun.

Life Cycle of Plants — Flower Power

As they grow, most plants produce flowers. Flowers don't just look pretty – they help the plant to **reproduce** by making seeds.

Flowering plants need to be **pollinated** in order for seeds to grow. This involves moving the powdery stuff called pollen from a male part of one flower (the anther) to a female part of another (the stigma).

Insects, birds and bats are brilliant **pollinators**. As they visit flowers to drink the **nectar**, they move the pollen around to all the right places. Then seeds can start to form.

Super Stems

But not all plants need to be pollinated to reproduce. Some, like spider plants, grow special stems called runners. A whole new plant can grow from a runner.

Life Cycle of Plants — Survival Kit

Plants need water, light, air and nutrients to survive. Most get their nutrients from the soil. A few also eat insects. Yep, you read that right. Plants can be **carnivores**!

This plant is called a Venus fly trap. Can you see what's inside?

Water

Light and air

Nutrients

= Life

Light energy from the sun helps plants to make their own food. Temperature is important to plants too. Heat from the sun helps them grow, but if they get too hot they might wilt and die. If they get too cold, they could freeze.

Plant Givers   Breathe Easy

Plants have so much to offer humans and all types of creatures. They are like the most generous gift-givers ever! They provide air, food, shelter, clothes and even medicine.

Plants breathe like humans do. But while humans breathe in oxygen and breathe out carbon dioxide, plants do the opposite! This means plants are very important to humans. Without them, there wouldn't be enough oxygen to breathe.

Cutting down wide areas of trees is called deforestation.

Timber from tree trunks is used to build all sorts of things, from homes and boats to toys and playgrounds. But trees are precious and take many years to grow, so it's important to replace the ones that are chopped down.

Plant Givers — Food for Thought

The seeds, fruits and leaves that a plant produces can be used as food for humans and animals.

Fruit, vegetables, rice and bread all come from plants. Even foods like meat, eggs and cheese depend on plants, because the animals that produce them need to eat plants to survive.

Roots can be edible too. Fancy a carrot?

Many humans love sugary foods like chocolate, biscuits and cake. Guess where sugar comes from? That's right – it's a plant!

Sugar Cane

When animals poo out the food they've eaten, it goes back into the earth as manure – full of nutrients that plants love to grow in. The life cycle keeps spinning!

Fitting In — Adaptation

Over many thousands of years, plants have learnt to fit in with their surroundings. This process is called adaptation, which means plants are able to change in ways that help them survive in all types of **habitat**.

Cacti store water in their fleshy leaves. This allows them to live in dry places like deserts.

A cactus can live over a year without rain!

Airplant

Airplants grow in damp conditions such as rainforests. Because there is so much moisture in the air, they absorb water through their leaves instead of their roots.

Mistletoe attaches itself to another plant, usually a tall tree, and takes water and nutrients from the 'host' tree.

Mistletoe

Fitting In   Watery Wonders

Not all plants grow on land. Many live in ponds, lakes or the sea. Ocean plants like seagrass have adapted to grow in salty water. Lots of sea creatures rely on these plants for their food, from the tiniest fish to larger animals such as manatees.

Plants that grow in fresh water often have colourful flowers that bloom above the surface of a lake or pond. Waterlilies have large, round leaves that give shade and protection for fish. The leaves also make perfect landing pads for frogs and dragonflies!

Even in the harshest of **climates**, plants have adapted their life cycles to suit different **environments**. Under the Arctic snow, tiny plants wait in sub-zero temperatures. When the snow melts during the brief Arctic summer, these tough plants grab their chance to bloom.

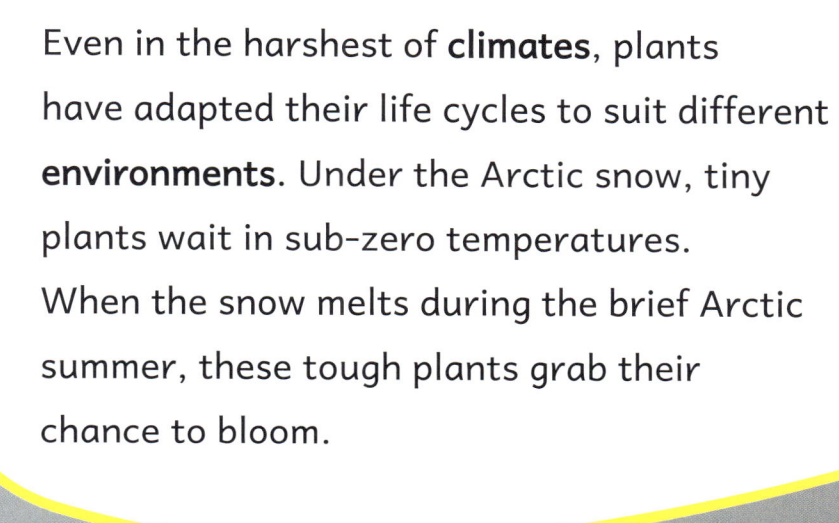

MESSAGE SENT

Dear Peebs and Pob,

Plants on Earth have amazing lives that benefit the whole planet. Whatever the climate, they will try to find a way to grow.

From the tiniest daisy to the largest tree, every plant is precious. It's no wonder humans need to protect their green world!

From,
Finn and Zeek x

The Redwood - the tallest plant species on Earth.

Quiz

1. How many different types of plant are thought to grow on Earth?
a) 800
b) 96
c) Nearly 400,000

2. Which part of the plant grows down into the soil?
a) Leaves
b) Roots
c) Flower

3) Which is a carnivorous plant?
a) Venus Fly Trap
b) Mars Spider Trap
c) Venus Bug Catcher

4. What is germination?
a) When roots and shoots start to grow from a seed
b) When rain falls on a plant
c) When insects drink nectar

5. What is the name of a male part of a flower?
a) Petal
b) Anther
c) Stigma

6. What kind of air do plants breathe in?
a) Carbon dioxide
b) Helium
c) Oxygen

Turn over for answers

Index/Glossary

Carnivores pg 14

A carnivore is a plant or animal that eats other animals.

Climates pg 25

The weather conditions usually found in a particular place over a long period of time.

Environment pg 25

The natural surroundings in which a plant, person or animal lives.

Germination pg 10

This is when a seed starts to grow into a new plant by sprouting roots and shoots.

Habitat pg 20

The habitat of an animal or plant is the natural environment in which it normally lives or grows.

Quiz Answers:
1. c, 2. b, 3. a, 4. a, 5. b, 6. a

Nectar pg 12

A sweet liquid made by flowers. Nectar is collected by insects, birds and other animals.

Nutrients pg 9, 14, 15, 21

Nutrients are the goodness that plants need to absorb to grow properly. Most nutrients, such as minerals, are found in the soil.

Pollinated/pollination pg 12, 13

When pollen is transferred from the male part of a flower to the female part, pollination takes place. Once a plant is pollinated, it can make seeds.

Pollinators pg 12

These are the insects, birds and other creatures that help to transfer pollen from one flower to another.

Reproduce pg 12, 13

This means to make babies or seeds. Most plants reproduce by making seeds, which grow into new plants.

Book Bands for Guided Reading

The Institute of Education book banding system is a scale of colours that reflects the various levels of reading difficulty. The bands are assigned by taking into account the content, the language style, the layout and phonics. Word, phrase and sentence level work is also taken into consideration.

Maverick Early Readers are a bright, attractive range of books covering the pink to white bands. All of these books have been book banded for guided reading to the industry standard and edited by a leading educational consultant.

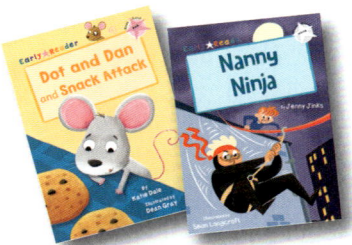

Fiction

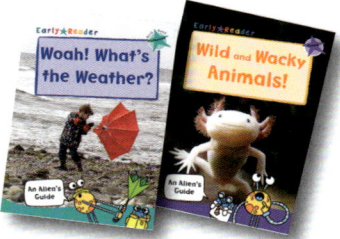

Non-fiction

To view the whole Maverick Readers scheme, visit our website at www.maverickearlyreaders.com

Or scan the QR code above to view our scheme instantly!